Princess Isabella
and
The Mystery of the Golden Keys

K. B. Lebsock & Jessica Wulf

PRINCESS ISABELLA
and
THE MYSTERY OF THE GOLDEN KEYS

K. B. LEBSOCK & JESSICA WULF

Joshua Tree Publishing
• Chicago •

JoshuaTreePublishing.com

ISBN: 978-1-941049-01-3

Copyright © 2015 K. B. Lebsock and Jessica Wulf
All rights reserved. No part of this book may be reproduced or transmitted in any form or by any means, electronic or mechanical, including photocopying, recording or by any information storage and retrieval system without written permission from the authors.

Photography: K. B. Lebsock

Printed in the United States of America

ACKNOWLEDGEMENTS

We would like to express our gratitude to the participants in this book. We appreciate their time, energy and patience given to this project. It was fun working with everyone.

Teacher: Ms Amber Reed; Students: Keegan McCorkle, Gavin Ritmaha, Saul Mendez, Yasmin Mercado, Aidan Chung, Marc Padilla, Zane Martinez, Adrianna Tejada, Quint Morgan; Kathleen Stiny and Gracie; Tanya Smetana, hair dresser; Donny Legino, owner of Legino Diamonds; Deanna Kordes, owner of Ritzy Rover Pet Boutique & Spa; The Corporal: Corporal Paul VonFeldt; The Dentist: Jim Duff; The Trainer: Troy Huseby, owner of Swing Physical Therapy (Glendale, AZ); Isabel Raley; Airplane Cessna 172: Mark Hochstedler– learntoflydenver.com; Motorcycle Rider: Shawn Massa and Peter; Miner: Will Frey and friends Cora and Elias Rosenberg; Zuma's Rescue Ranch (Littleton,CO); Zoo Friend: Trinity Anderson; Gorilla: Donny Legino. Boardroom Doggie friends: Sandy Urbanic - Domino, Karen Ann Allard - QT Bear, Sarah Gilsdorf - Chica, Donna Taylor - Beau, Mandy & Roxie, and Kathleen Stiny - Gracie; Woodley's Fine Furniture, High Plains Stone Company, and Collegiate Peaks Bank.

A BIG THANK YOU TO ALL!!!

PRINCESS ISABELLA
and
THE MYSTERY OF THE GOLDEN KEYS

Classes were starting soon, so Princess Isabella stopped by school to register and get her class assignments.

All of her classmates and the teacher were there.
One by one, with a smile, each handed her a key.
Her teacher was the last to give her a key, and then
she said, "We want you to have these Golden Keys,
and one day you will know what they are for,
so you must be patient."
Well, Isabella thought that was very odd, but she
accepted the keys, registered for the school year,
and got her list of classes.

Back at home, Isabella noticed that everyone had keys. They did not wear them or carry them all the time, but they had one or more keys. Even Gracie, Isabella's doggie friend, was fascinated with the key her mom wore.

Now Isabella had keys, too. What did they mean? Then she realized the meaning of the keys was a mystery! Isabella had a mystery to solve!!!

IT WAS TIME TO GET TO WORK!!!

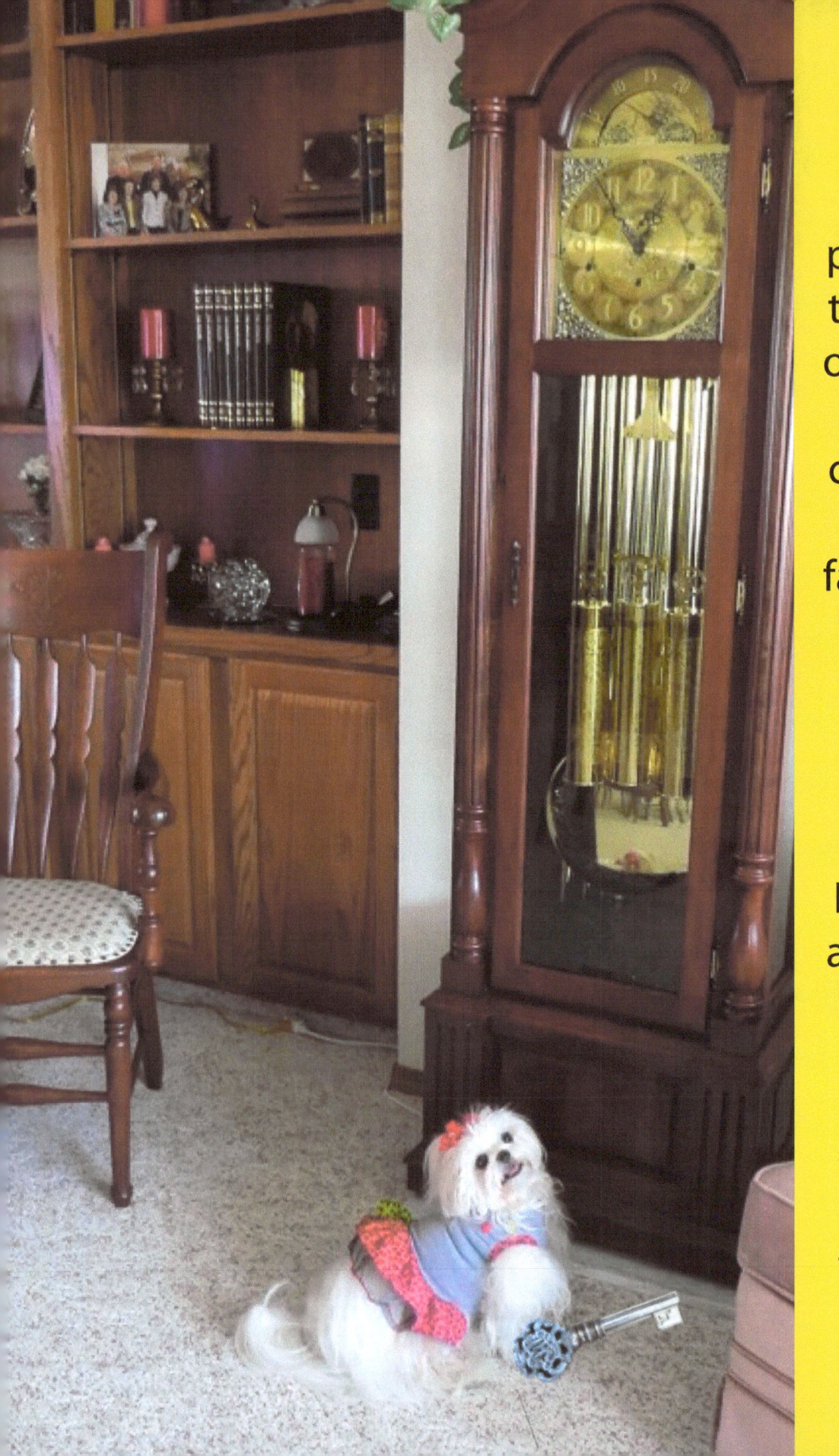

Right there in the den was a good place to start: the great big, old-fashioned grandfather clock needed an old-fashioned key to open the glass door and wind the clock. Full of hope, Isabella tried all of her keys on the clock case door, but none worked. She wondered: Where to go from there?

Princess Isabella decided to continue her investigation into the mystery of the keys by going to the shops in her neighborhood. Perhaps she would get some ideas of what the keys could be used for.

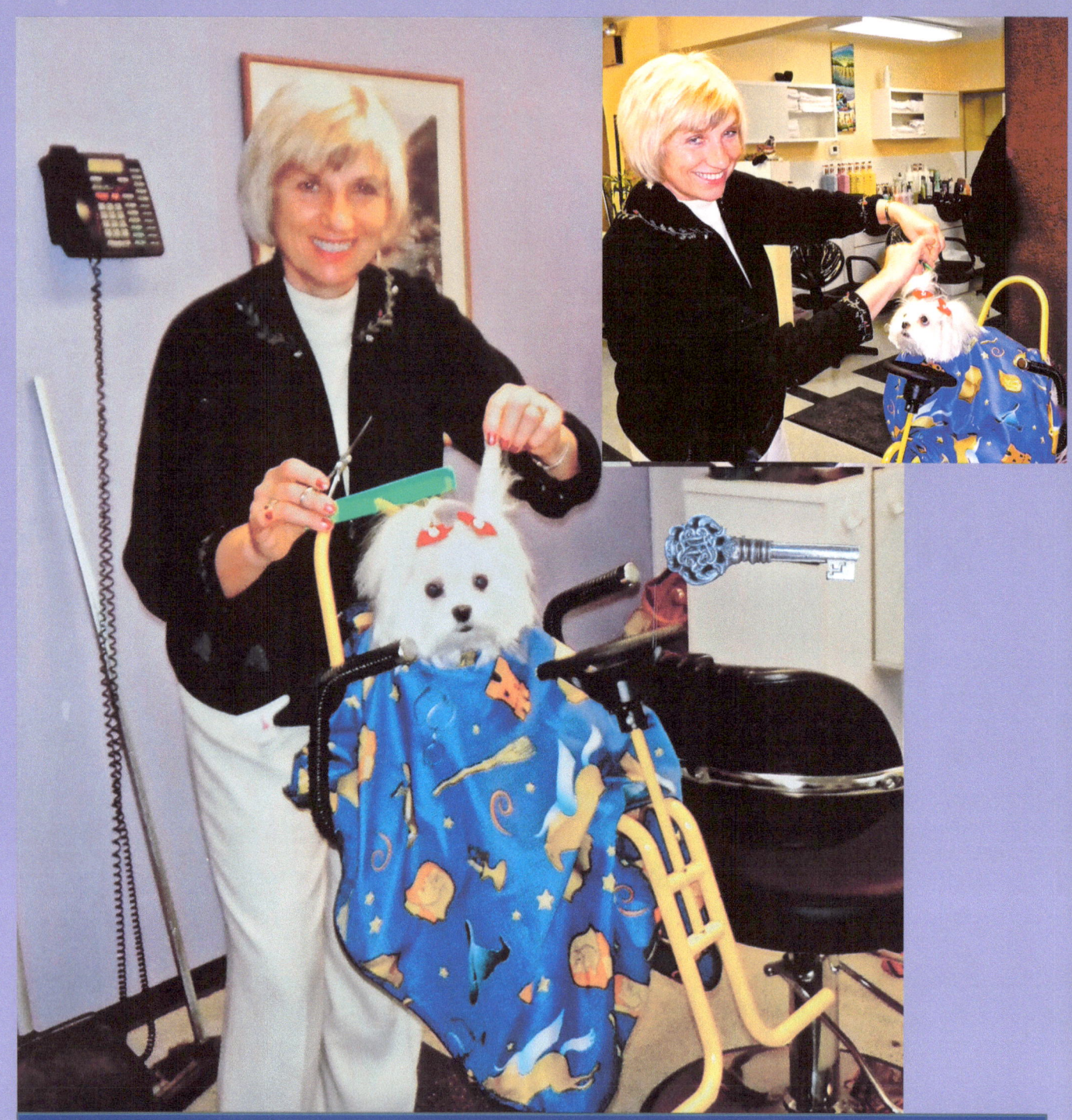

Her first stop was at the Beauty Salon, where Tanya fixed her hair real pretty. Rather than offer any clues to the meaning of the keys Isabella already had, Tanya gave her another key with no explanation.
HOW STRANGE!!!

Her next stop was at the neighborhood jewelry store, where she saw lots of pretty, shiny jewelry. Princess Isabella told Donny, the jeweler, she had been given a few Golden Keys and did not know what they opened. Donny suggested she try her keys in a beautiful jewelry box that sat on the counter.

The box was very pretty,
but none of the keys fit in the lock.

Donny said he hoped she found what she was looking for. Then, to Isabella's surprise, he gave her another key. OH, NO! ! !
Now Isabella had another key she didn't know what to do with! ! !

Princess Isabella stopped next at her favorite store, Ritzy Rover. Her primary mission, of course, was to search for answers about the Golden Keys, but she also wanted to shop!

She had fun playing with the amazing assortment of toys and found several possibilities for a new dress and then, Deanna gave her yet another key!!!

NOW WHAT?
Isabella wondered.

Princess Isabella had a friend at the police station, which was right across the street. Surely the Corporal would have some ideas for her. It was his job, after all, to solve mysteries!

Isabella waited for the walk signal at the crosswalk and hurried to the station. She told the Corporal about her collection of keys and asked him for ideas. He explained that police cell doors no longer used keys because computers opened and closed the doors, so he didn't think he had an answer for her. Then, he pulled an old key from his desk drawer and gave it to her. OH, NO! ! ! But Isabella was gracious and accepted the key with thanks. She left the station more puzzled than ever.

On the way home, Isabella remembered she had a dental check-up appointment. Her family always made sure her teeth were in good condition and she knew the appointment was important. She decided to ask Jim, her kind dentist, if he had any ideas about the keys.

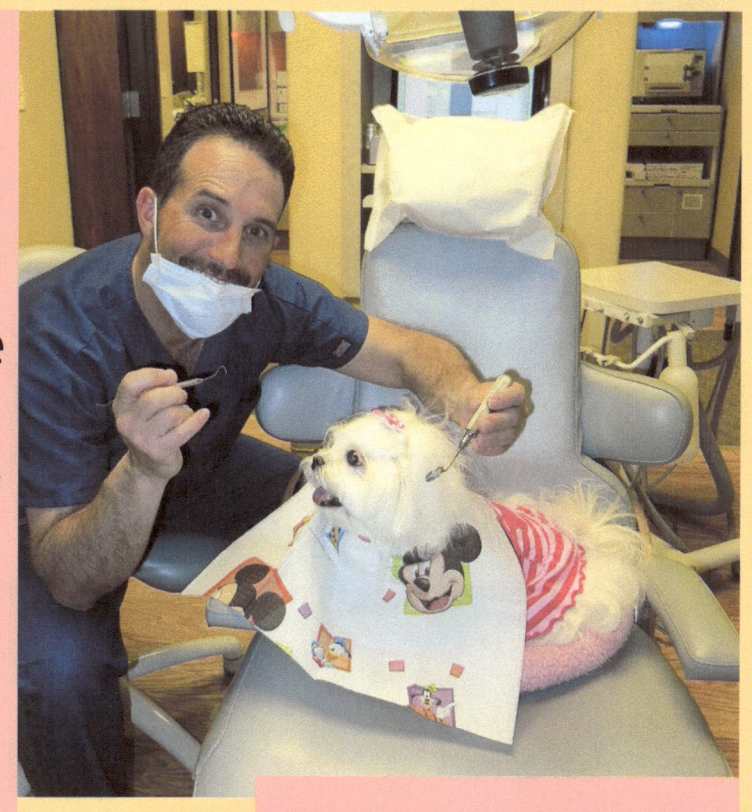

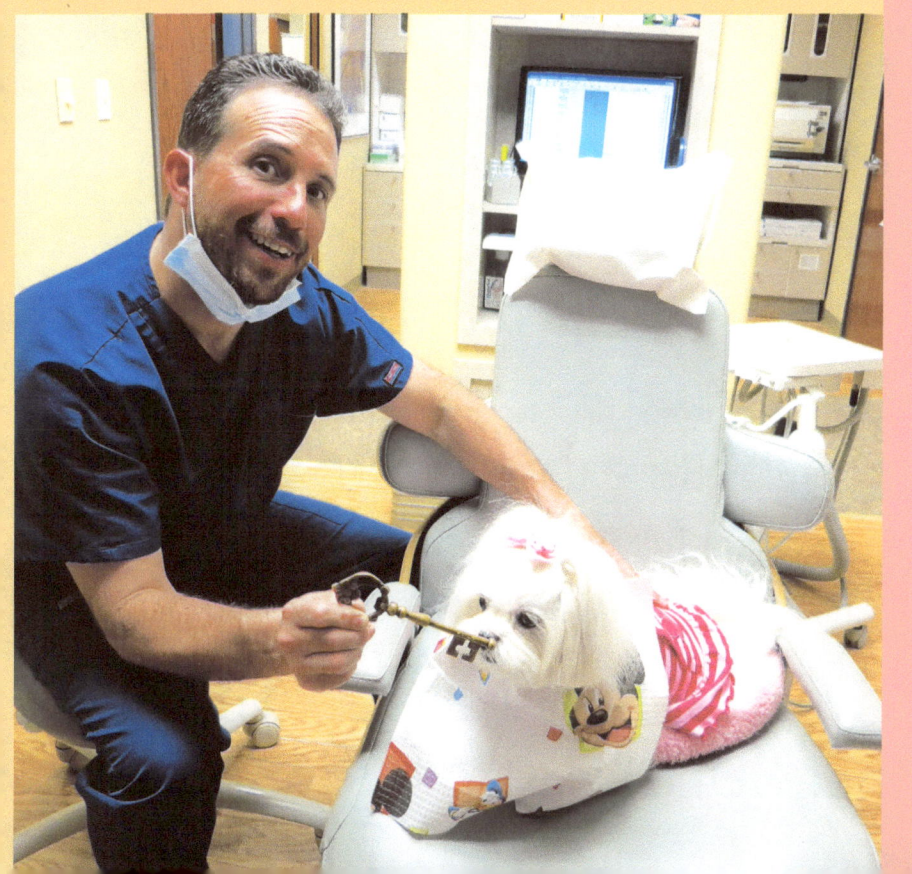

He had no answers. Then, to complicate things even more, he gave her another key!!! This mystery solving was making Isabella tired, so she decided to do what all wise doggies do when they are tired: TAKE A NAP!!!

After her nap, Princess Isabella felt refreshed and energetic, so she went to the gym. While on the exercise machine, Isabella explained to Troy, her personal trainer, the Mystery of the Keys.

Troy had no answers for her AND he gave her another GOLDEN KEY!!!

Isabella passed the Post Office next and remembered that there were lots of boxes in the Post Office, boxes that all needed keys to open them! She decided to ask her friends, Isabel and Molly, to help her check all of the keys in the locks of all those boxes. Surely at least one of Isabella's keys would open at least one Post Office box. Maybe there was a treasure inside!

The little team got to work. They tried all of the keys in all of the boxes, which took a very long time. None of the keys fit any of the boxes. They were disappointed, but they all agreed it was still fun solving mysteries, even when it was hard. Now it was time for Isabel and Molly to go home, and they wished Isabella good luck on her quest.

Isabella decided to go home, too, and do some research on Golden Keys. She didn't find any answers, but she did get some ideas of where to search next. By now it was late. Better to get a good night's sleep and start fresh in the morning. At least she'd know where to start because she made a list.

The next morning, Princess Isabella looked at her list and decided to go to the car dealership first. None of her keys started any of the cars, but Isabella really enjoyed pretending to drive a beautiful new Corvette.

THE PERFECT CAR FOR A PRINCESS!!!

One of her friends had told Isabella about her dad's airplane, a SKYHAWK II, and Isabella knew that a key was needed to start airplanes. She put on her WWII-era Royal Flight Bomber Jacket.
(These jackets were worn by the British Royal Air Force.)

Isabella wore hers only when flying.

At the airport, she found the plane on the tarmac. WOW! Even for a small plane, the step up was a BIG one.

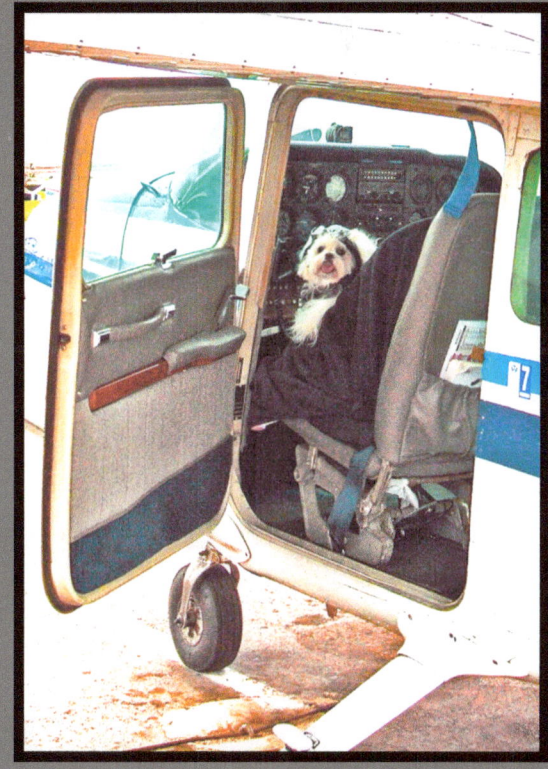

Isabella tried all of her keys, but none started the engine. In case that happened, her friend had given her a key made especially for this plane, so she decided to take a flight.
She had a GREAT TIME!

After her plane ride, the next place on her list was a great big locked gate at a fancy building not far away, so she called her friends, Shawn and Peter, and asked for their help. They came and picked her up on Shawn's super-fast motorcycle. None of the keys opened the gate. Shawn told her about Will, a miner who had found a treasure chest in an old mine. Isabella thought it was worth a try, so Shawn dropped her off.

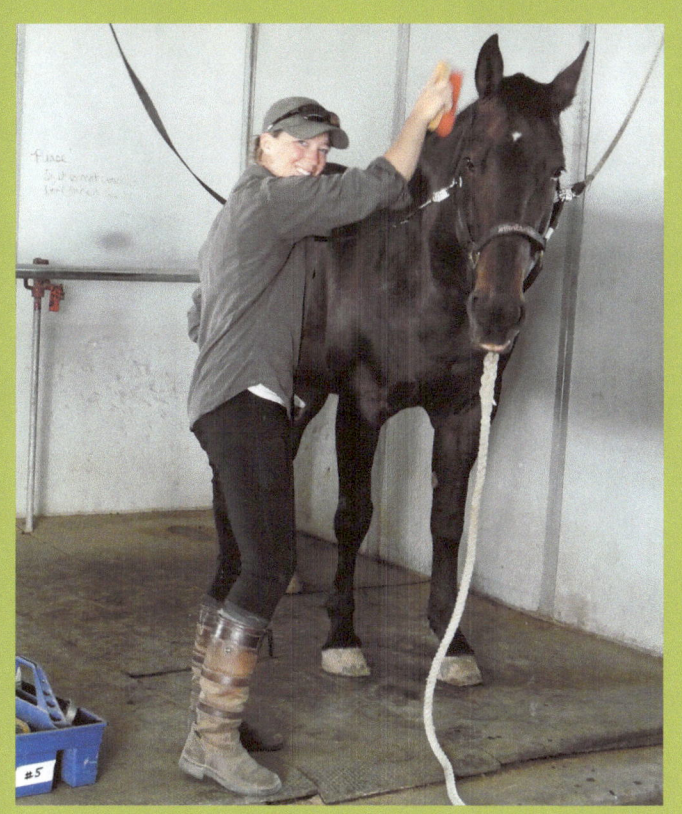

Isabella realized that she was not far from the next place on her list: a stable where her friends Zoie, a beautiful Morgan horse, and Katie lived. Isabella explained the keys, and Katie suggested they try the keys in the big lock on Zoie's corral gate. Katie saddled Zoie and they all went to the gate.

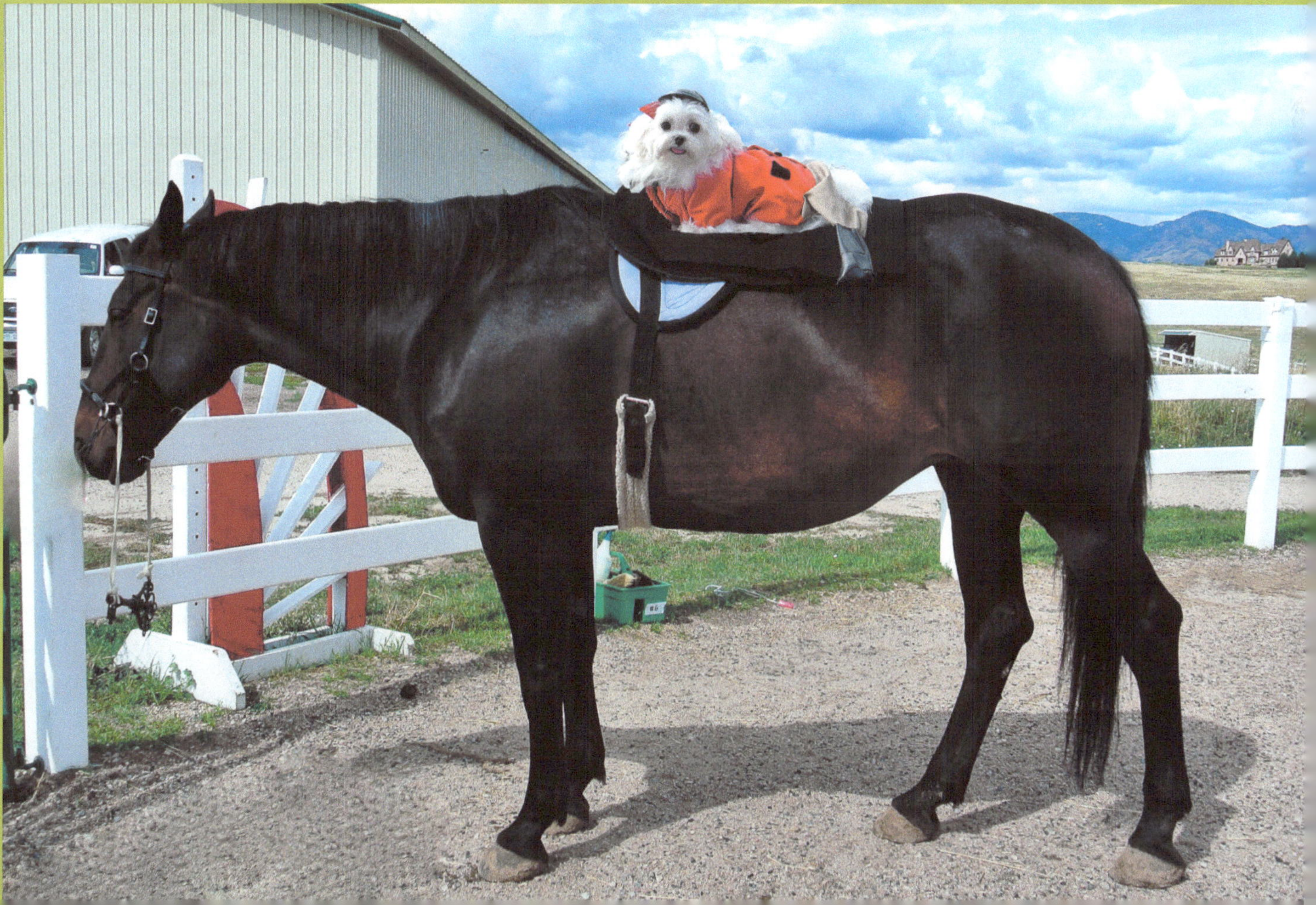

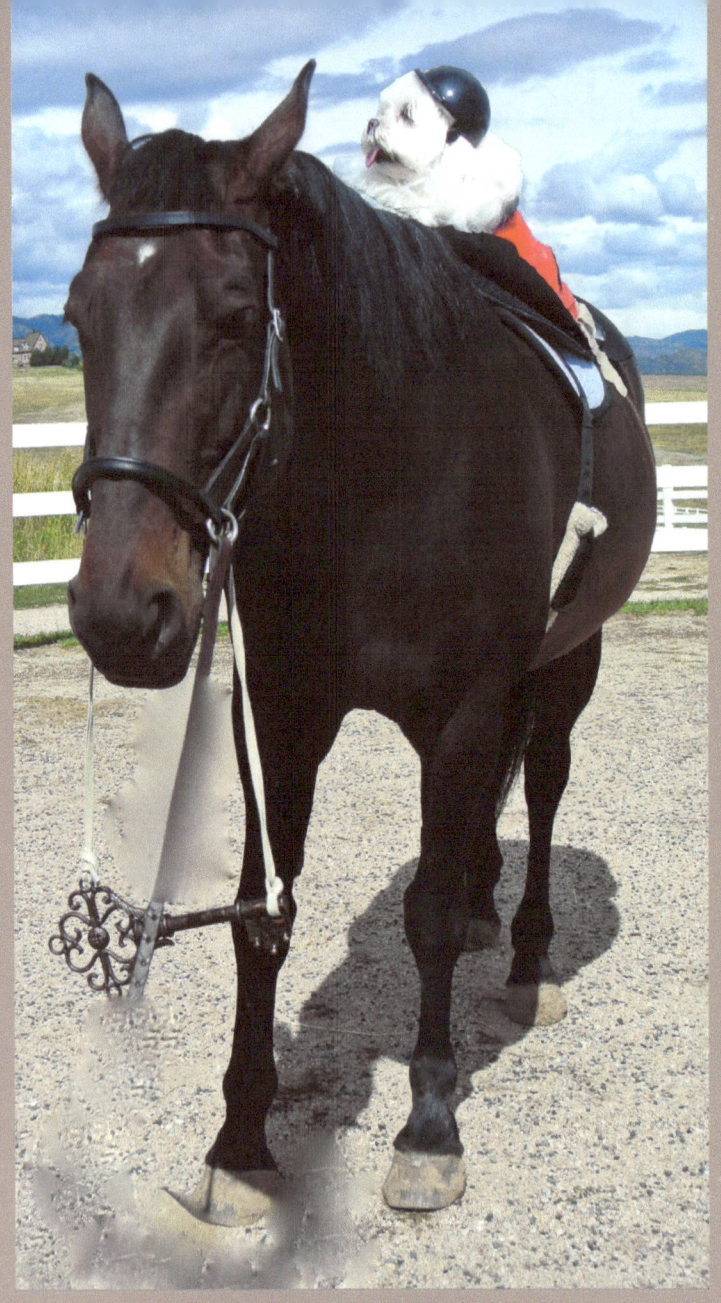

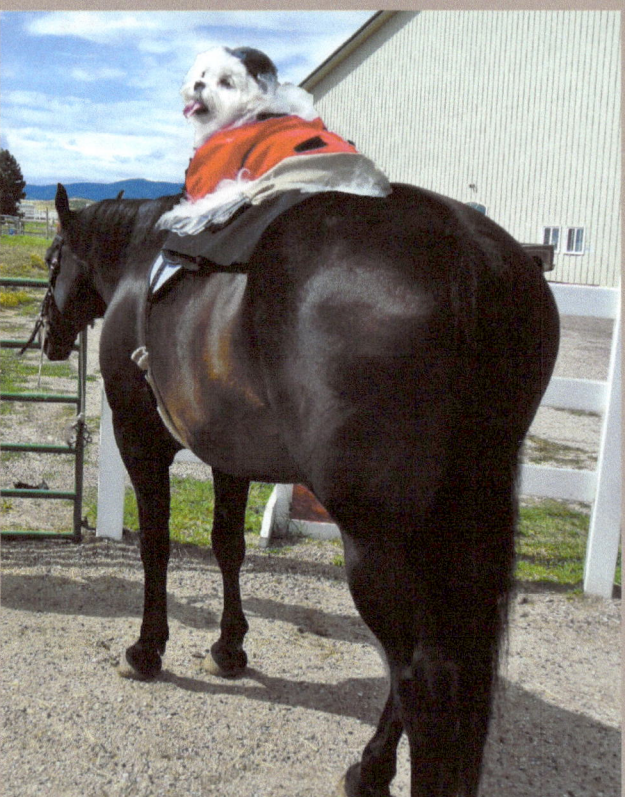

Again it happened! None of the keys would open the lock.

However, Isabella enjoyed her ride with Zoie. She was having a good time even without solving the mystery! Isabella then left to meet her friend Trinity, who had offered to help.

Katie took off the saddle, and Zoie returned to the pasture to munch some grass and relax.

Isabella arrived at the front gate of the Denver Zoo and played with a lion cub for a few minutes, then went to find Trinity.

They met at a big black iron fence that looked very strong. Isabella was glad the fence was so strong, because behind that fence was a very large and fierce-looking gorilla! The locked gate was nearby, but Isabella and Trinity agreed that even if one of the keys worked, it would be a BAD IDEA to open that gate! The gorilla came up to the fence and grabbed two bars. Isabella and Trinity both jumped back, expecting the gorilla would growl at them.

Instead, the gorilla told them her name was Tilla and asked if they would each like a banana! How nice of Tilla! The sign on the fence said "Do Not Feed the Gorilla," but it didn't say anything about the gorilla feeding them.

So Isabella and Trinity accepted the bananas. At least Tilla didn't give them a key!!!

After the adventure at the zoo, Isabella found out that Isabel and Molly had invited her for a sleep over.

Isabel thought that maybe one of Isabella's keys might fit the lock on her diary. Isabella packed her monkey jammies and joined her friends. None of the keys fit in the diary lock, so they read their books for a while, then went to sleep. Isabella dreamed of keys all night long.

The next morning, Princess Isabella had an idea. If she called a board meeting of all her doggie friends, maybe they could help her brainstorm the mystery of the keys, and maybe they would come up with some new ideas. They all watched as Isabella's assistant entered the room with the keys.

The keys were meant to be gifts to loved ones! That was what her teacher had wanted her to learn! That was why all of her classmates, and Tanya the hair dresser, and Donny the jeweler, and Deanna the store owner, and the police Corporal, and Jim the dentist, and Troy the trainer, had given her keys. They all cared about Isabella and wanted her to know!

THE KEYS WERE TO THEIR HEARTS! ! !

The Mystery of the Golden Keys was solved!

Now it was Princess Isabella's turn to give the keys to her heart away to her beloved friends. All the doggies loved receiving a key from Princess Isabella, and they promised to carry on the lovely tradition by one day giving their keys away to those they loved.

THE END

Another Princess Isabella Adventure
Princess Isabella
and
The Mystery of the Pink Dragon

From her birthplace in Wyoming to her forever-home in Colorado, Princess Isabella leads a seemingly charmed life with people and friends who adore her. Then her happy life gets even better when she discovers in her doggie bed a new friend. Isabella and Pink Dragon soon become Best Friends. They go everywhere together and each night they snuggle under the froggie blanket to sleep. But then one day something mysterious and terrible happens: Pink Dragon disappears. And so begins Isabella's search for her dear friend.

The Mystery of the Pink Dragon
ISBN: 978-0-9886577-7-9

Princess Isabella is an accomplished Dog Dancer and a member of three performing Dog Dance Groups with numerous public performances to her credit.

The Mystery of the Golden Keys is the second mystery she has solved.

Princess Isabella Website:
MyPrincessIsabella.com

The Authors

 **K. B. Lebsock** lives in Colorado. She has a B.A. from Loretto Heights College and enjoys ballet, classical music, BBC TV dramas, and photography, which is why her camera goes with her everywhere. She has a deep love for animals of all kinds. *Princess Isabella and the Mystery of the Golden Keys* is her second book. Author Website: **KBLebsock.com**

 **Jessica Wulf** is a native of North Dakota but has spent most of her life in Colorado, where she now lives with her husband and six happy dogs. She has a B.A. in History and has published six historical fiction novels. *Princess Isabella and the Mystery of the Golden Keys* is her second children's book. Author Website: **JessicaWulf.com**

www.ingramcontent.com/pod-product-compliance
Lightning Source LLC
Chambersburg PA
CBHW050758110526
44588CB00002B/44